Old PORTADOWN

by

Alex F. Young, with photographs from the Des Quail collection

St Mark's Church Sunday school outing makes its way down High Street towards the railway station in the days before the First World War. The only surviving building on this part of the street is the Belfast Bank, now Anglia House. Next door on the right was Anderson the draper and undertaker. Having served his time as a clerk with William Paul & Sons, the High Street milliner and draper, Anderson opened this business with his wife working as seamstress. A native of Portadown, and a town councillor for many years, he died in 1941 aged eighty-seven years. Miss McBroom the grocer was supplied with fresh milk from two cows she kept in the yard behind her shop. Cordner, whose bicycle shop is on the far right, was an engineer who, perhaps, ultimately wasted his talents. He is remembered for having a hand in the design of the first machine gun synchronized to fire through an aircraft propeller and was also one of the first men in Britain to fly.

ACKNOWLEDGEMENTS
The author wishes to thank the people of Portadown for their assistance, in particular Brian Courtney and David Armstrong of the Portadown Times, Billy Hannah, Joe Hughes, Rodney Magowan, Ernest Thornton, Harry Murphy and the Royal British Legion, Robbie Clarke and Portadown Boat Club, Greg Forbes, Sam Hewitt, Jim Lyttle (www.portadownphotos. freehomepage.com), Hilda Winter, William Kilpatrick and Portadown Golf Club, Mrs P.M. Irwin, Mrs Dorothy Livingstone, Sam Forbes, Jim Kane, Michael Johnston, Maureen McAdam, Elizabeth Watson, David Uprichard, Jim Sprott, Paddy Judge, George Sharkey, Rosemary Calvert, Arthur Chapman, R. David Jones, Harry Welsh and Bill Broadhurst (who provided information about the fire brigade), Rev. John A Pickering, Portadown Library, and the Ulster Folk and Transport Museum.

FURTHER READING
The books listed below were used by the author during his research. None of them are available from Stenlake Publishing. Those interested in finding out more are advised to contact their local bookshop or reference library.

Craigavon Historical Society, *Portadown Trail*, no date.

E.M. Patterson, *The Great Northern Railway of Ireland*, no date.

Portadown Cultural Heritage Committee, *The Orange Citadel*, 1996.

Rotary Club of Portadown, *Portadown*, no date.

Southern Education & Library Board, *Portadown – An Introductory History*, 1995.

Market Street, Portadown. (283).

This view of High Street from the corner of Thomas Street shows the taxi rank which gave planners the idea of a central reservation. Burnett the draper and haberdasher, which rounded the corner from Woodhouse Street, is now premises of the Halifax Building Society, and gone are the buildings which neighboured the surviving Bank of Ireland building which dates from 1868. In the foreground the ever patient horse awaits the return of the driver of Portadown Laundry's delivery cart.

INTRODUCTION

For a town destined to become Ireland's 'Hub of the North' with the coming of the railways, Portadown was a late starter – the name first appearing in 1609 as *Ballywarren al Portadowne*. Some say the name derives from *Port-ne-Dun* ('Port of the Fortress'), while others argue for 'Port of Down', a reference to the then strategic ferry crossing over the River Bann. Title deeds from 1660 refer to it as 'King's Ferry'.

With the Plantation of Ulster in 1610, King James I granted 2,000 acres of land to an English landowner, part of which, along the west bank of the River Bann, was eventually bought, after passing through many hands, by Michael Obins. Within ten years he had built a castle, 'a good house of brick and lime for himself and settled twenty tenants who, with their undertenants, were able to muster forty-six men with arms'. Recalled in the name Castle Street, Obins' property included the present Peoples Park. Obins Castle would be a casualty of the Civil War when it was sacked by General Owen Roe O'Neill in June 1641. O'Neill was also responsible for the massacre of settlers who were shot or drowned in the Bann.

In 1703 Anthony Obins, great-grandson of Michael, recognised the River Bann's importance as a trade route and commissioned a survey for the future Newry to Lough Neagh canal. Completed in 1741, this trading conduit opened Portadown to the world. The canal ran to Lough Neagh from where the Lagan Canal formed a route to the sea via Belfast. The first summit level waterway in Britain, the Newry Canal's fourteen locks elevate it at Poyntzpass to 78 feet above sea level.

Anthony's grandson, Michael Obins, won parliamentary petitions for a linen market in 1762 and a grain market, which would handle 5,000 tons of wheat per annum, in 1780. In the rich arable land around Portadown, grain, vegetables, linen and fruit were grown – cider production being an early success – which now found a wider market. Equally, cargoes of stone and timber for building, and coal to fire the future mills, kept the barges busy.

With the opening of the Ulster Railway's line from Belfast, the railway arrived in September 1842; it had reached Seagoe in January that year and would go on to Armagh six years later when the Bann was bridged. The opening of the line from Portadown to Dublin in 1855 was followed by extensions to Dungannon and Omagh. The town was now the 'Hub of the North' and, apart from oiling the wheels of commerce, the benefits to the local people were enormous. By 1859 a Portadown family could take the 3rd class day return trip to Belfast for one shilling (5p).

Industrialisation arrived in the town in the form of the power loom and the weaving factories of Watson, Armstrong, Acheson, the Castle Island Linen Company, and Grimshaw & McFadden. It also brought unemployment as it effectively killed off the cottage weaving industry and halved the town's workforce to 2,000. However, from the early 1880s the blossoming hemstitch industry grew with Dawson, Hamilton & Robb, Gilbert at Seagoe, Samuel Wilson at Alma Terrace and others employing over 600 in the manufacture of linen handkerchiefs, pillow cases, shams and lawn. Portadown, along with Lurgan and Lisburn, became the centre of the British linen industry.

The canal helped the expansion of other businesses, both by bringing in raw materials such as wood for the sawmills of Bright Brothers, Collen Brothers and T.A. Shillington, and flax for the spinners, or in taking produce to distant markets, such as McCammon & Sprott's bacon and ham, and rope and twine from Logan's on Carrickblacker Road.

Throughout eighteenth century Britain, industrialisation wrought demographic changes as families moved to the expanding industrial centres. Portadown was no exception, transforming it from a rural village to what the novelist William Makepeace Thackeray described in 1842 as 'a brisk little town'. Another writer in the 1840s noted that ' . . . the thriving little town of Portadown . . . has a very superior trading position . . . the town though small, is wealthy and respectable and is noted for the spirit and enterprise of its merchants.' Between 1821 and 1851 the population doubled to just over 3,000, and in the following thirty years more than doubled again. The population in 1991 was 21,229.

The Irish (Union of Parishes) Act of 1827 created Portadown Town Commissioners who had responsibility for cleansing, sewerage, lighting, and the preservation of law and order with watchmen, the forerunner of today's police service. To finance this a levy was placed on each of the 170 houses in the town valued over £5. At its first meeting on 13 October 1828 Thomas Shillington was appointed chairman. From 1898 until 1947 an urban council managed the town's affairs before it reverted to borough status. The latest change came in 1973 when Lurgan joined Portadown under the city umbrella of Craigavon.

Portadown's days as the 'Hub of the North' are long gone, but the creation of Craigavon is finally paying dividends as it is now one of Northern Ireland's main manufacturing bases and is the third largest urban centre after Belfast and Londonderry. There is also much history to celebrate as the following pages show.

At the head of Market Street stands St Mark's Church (initially St Martin's), built of blackstone with sandstone dressings. Constructed at a cost of £1,300, it was consecrated on 14 November 1826 when Portadown was disjoined from Drumcree and created a parish in its own right. In use until 1809, the town's gallows had occupied the site. Various extensions and enlargements culminated in 1930 with the addition of the pinnacled bell tower which was added as a memorial to those lost in the First World War. The tower's foundation stone was laid on All Saints Day (1 November) 1928 by Mrs C.F. d'Arcy, the wife of His Grace, the Lord Primate of All Ireland. The statue on the right is of Colonel Sir Edward Saunderson MP (erected 1910), while on the left is the war memorial (erected 1925). The prominent white building along the left fork of Church Street, just before it becomes Armagh Road, is Fergus Hall. It bears the stone plaque with the legend 'Portadown National Schools – Rebuilt AD 1889' and dates from the 1840s when it was the Duke's School, named after the Duke of Manchester. It now serves as a hall to St Mark's Church. The bus in the foreground of this 1930s photograph carries an advertisement for Eakin the Jeweller who at that time was based in High Street.

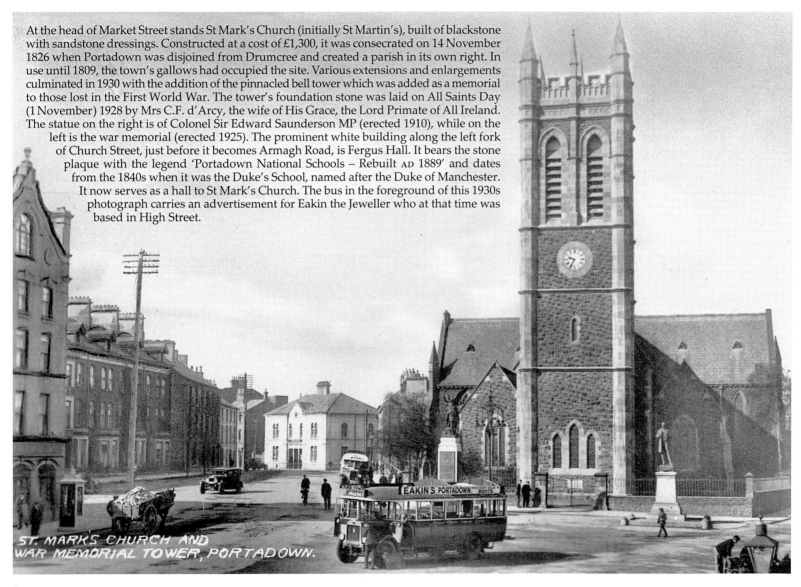

ST. MARK'S CHURCH AND
WAR MEMORIAL TOWER, PORTADOWN.

The High Street, pictured in the 1950s, looking towards Market Street and St Marks Church. The central reservation is in place, but even though motor cars mingled with horses and carts there was evidently still no need for yellow or white lines and the pelican crossing was still in the world of the ornithologist. The buildings on the right, running up from the Bank of Ireland, including Mason the grocer and Hipps the tailor, to Burnett's at the corner of Woodhouse Street were all swept away and replaced with structures of glass and steel.

Market Day in Portadown

Portadown was a market town with traditional days for pork, fowl, butter, eggs and potatoes. The opening of the canals in the eighteenth century brought produce and goods from far beyond its own fertile fields. Not surprisingly the main venue was Market Street, pictured here from the tower of St Mark's Church in the early 1900s. In 1878 the Duke of Manchester had granted the town's commissioners a 999 year lease for their markets and new buildings to house them were eventually erected between Market Street and William Street.

MARKET DAY, PORTADOWN.

The remnants of a Saturday morning clothing market on High Street, pictured up to the corner with Edward Street around 1914. Behind the stalls are Burnett the draper, Richardson's veterinary supplies, Walsh the seed merchant, and Twinem the gent's outfitters. At the end of the row is Miss Hall's Imperial Hotel which had a popular mirrored bar. Eakin's shoe store stands on the corner of Edward Street and beyond it was Montgomery the grocer and tea merchant and Paul's drapery store.

Fruit Market in Portadown

Traditionally the fruit market was held in William Street, but here it is pictured in High Street in the late 1920s. As a fruit growing area, the market would have been busiest in the autumn when up to 300 loads of apples could be on sale. By the time of this picture motor lorries were starting to displace the horse and cart.

742/34 Market Street, Portadown

By 1934 the horse and cart had finally lost out to the 'horseless carriage' as this view of Market Street shows. On the north side of the street were many businesses which in time would also disappear – Twinem Jackson's furniture store, McAnallen the chemist, Kelly's Bar, Rountree and Hewitt the grocer, and A.L. Martin's Market Pharmacy. The postcard from which this photograph comes bears the message: 'My cousin Sarah Cairns (née Macauley) lives there [Portadown]. Sarah has a family of two girls and two boys. Both girls, Virginia and Daisy, are married.' Does anybody know what became of this family?

What today's environmental health inspector would see as a nightmare and the freezer salesman a dream come true was the butcher's traditional way of displaying poultry and meat, particularly in the days up to Christmas. This photograph from the early 1920s shows Totton's shop at the corner of Market Street and Thomas Street in the premises later occupied by Maypole the grocer.

The lower part of 1930s High Street running onto Bridge Street and beyond. This unusual view of the street may have been photographed from a power pole, but at least Hipps the tailor was prepared for the publicity.

Started in Glasgow in 1883 by the Scottish businessman Sir William Smith, the Boys' Brigade movement came to Northern Ireland in 1888 when the 1st Belfast Company was formed. Between 1900 and 1902 it raised only a brief interest in Portadown. However, when the Boys' Life Brigade and the Boys' Brigade amalgamated at national level in 1926, there were seventy-five companies (and 4,600 members) and Portadown had three – 1st Portadown Company (of the Thomas Street Methodist Church), 2nd Company (Edenderry Presbyterian), and 3rd Company (St Mark's Church). This photograph, thought to be from the 1920s, shows the town's companies on parade as a part of a larger occasion or celebration. Only one lad has been identified – between the two girls on the left stands Norman Little, a future captain of 1st Company, whose family stayed in Bridge Street next to Moffatt the photographer.

The Belfast Bank, which opened in Portadown in the 1850s, was still flourishing when Anderson's drapery store closed in 1919 and reopened as Woolworth's 3d and 6d Store on 21 February 1921. Some years ago Woolworth's had 1,300 shops in Britain of which the Portadown branch was the ninety-third to open. Next to them was John Montgomery the undertaker, an active local politician who canvassed under the banner 'Vote for John Montgomery, the last man to let you down'.

If the boy cyclists were escorting the fire engine as outriders in this 1900 photograph we can assume (or hope) that it was not going to a fire! Portadown Volunteer Fire Brigade was founded by the town commissioners in 1850. Stationed in William Street, Captain Thomas Shillington and Lieutenant John Acheson had twelve volunteers under their charge and were equipped with a horse-drawn manual pump and a wheeled escape ladder. In 1956 the brigade moved to its present station in Thomas Street.

The Volunteer Fire Brigade at Ballyhannon Reservoir for the opening of the new water works in 1906, their brass and polish adding splendour to the occasion – which was probably what they were best at. Modern fire-fighting can blind us to how ineffectual the early, ill-equipped, fire service could be. A nineteenth century report of a fire in Portadown speaks of them arriving 'a day after the fire' and being unable to get the pump to work. Branded a nuisance, it was thought they would have been of as much service remaining in their shed.

Opened in 1909 by Professor Sir William Whitla MD, Thomas Street National School occupied the corner of Edward Street and Portmore Street. Mr J.A. Davidson was then principal. The original school building, opened in 1862, stands to its left. In 1934 the school was renamed Thomas Street Elementary and by 1950 was one of Portadown's seven elementary schools. Demolished in the early 1990s, it was replaced by the Wesley Hall and nursery school attached to Thomas Street Methodist Church. This was opened on 5 March 1994 by the Rev. Cecil A. Newell BD.

Coming to Portadown in 1882, the sisters of the Presentation Order set up a school in the old St Patrick's Parochial House in William Street. Initially it had a roll of eighty pupils. A new convent, pictured, opened in Thomas Street in July 1900 and the adjoining school opened the following March by which time the roll was 155. By 1948 it had 500 pupils. In 1967 the secondary department of 240 pupils transferred to the newly opened St Brigid's School. The convent building and school were converted to a housing complex of twenty-nine flats in 1996 and renamed Mourneview House.

Portadown had a reading room (above the Shambles [the slaughterhouse and flesh market] in William Street) from 1828, but as the twentieth century dawned the district council, seeing the need for modern premises, applied to Andrew Carnegie, the Scottish-born industrialist and philanthropist, to finance a full library. Carnegie agreed to gift £1,500 if the council provided the site. Choosing a plot in Edward Street, the red brick and stone building was almost finished for its opening on 1 August 1905. But it had none of the 6,500 books it was designed to hold and there was only £100 left in the coffers. The money raising concerts which went on for three more years finally filled the shelves. However, soon after opening another problem arose – men were monopolizing the library's newspapers, especially on Saturdays, for the racing and stock exchange news. The Anti-Gambling League, through the council, soon put a stop to that and ordered that the offending pages be removed from the papers each morning. In 2001 the library abandoned its Carnegie building for new premises in Church Street.

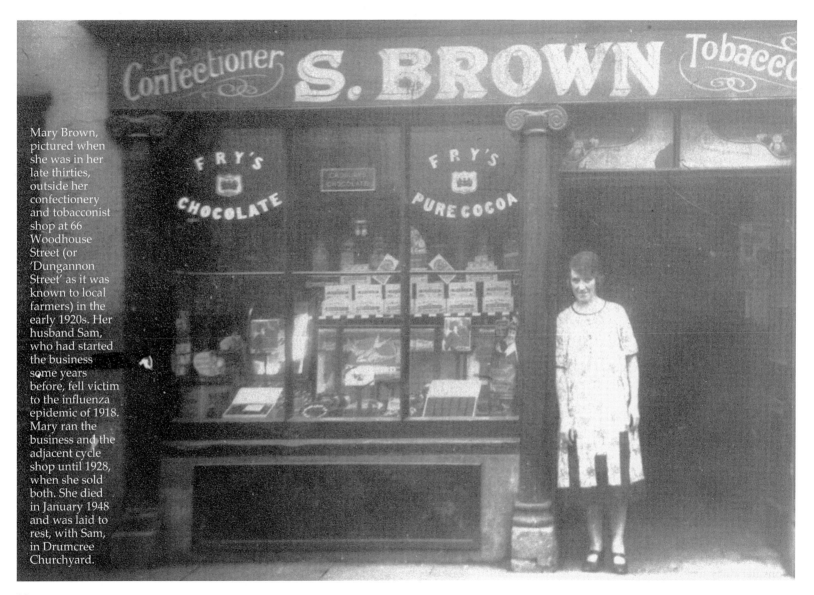

Mary Brown, pictured when she was in her late thirties, outside her confectionery and tobacconist shop at 66 Woodhouse Street (or 'Dungannon Street' as it was known to local farmers) in the early 1920s. Her husband Sam, who had started the business some years before, fell victim to the influenza epidemic of 1918. Mary ran the business and the adjacent cycle shop until 1928, when she sold both. She died in January 1948 and was laid to rest, with Sam, in Drumcree Churchyard.

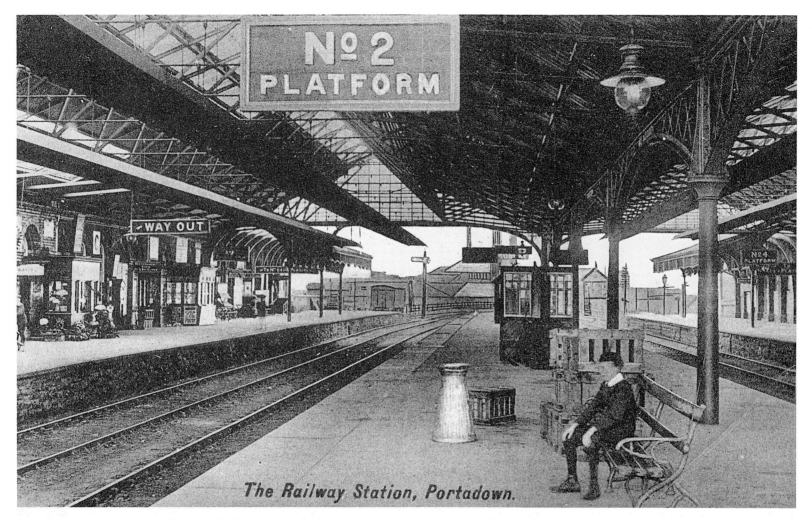

The Railway Station, Portadown.

This photograph of the Great Northern Railway Station in Watson Street captured an unusually quiet time, with no trains and only one waiting passenger and a milk churn. In its heyday, when Portadown was the 'Hub' of Northern Ireland's railway system, the station handled ninety trains per day. The beginning of the end came in 1957 with the closure of the Armagh line and was confirmed eight years later with the axing of the service to Londonderry. Soon afterwards the station was replaced by a commuter halt in Woodhouse Street.

Designed by Sir Henry Fowler, engine no. 74 'Dunluce Castle' was the eighteenth of its class (U2) and built in 1924 at Springburn, Glasgow, by the North British Locomotive Company at a cost of £5,328. By the time of its retiral in 1963 it had travelled 1,135,484 miles, mainly between Coleraine and Ballymena (although it spent the Second World War in service at York Road, Belfast). It was 50 feet and 8 inches in length and had a laden weight (including 5 tons of coal and 250 gallons of water) of 84 tons 9 cwt., all carried on 6 feet diameter wheels. Now restored, and in its North British crimson lake livery, it can be seen at the Ulster Folk and Transport Museum at Cultra. It is pictured here on the line near Portadown.

In this 1911 view of the Square, where High Street joins Castle Street on the left and Bridge Street on the right, stands the brick and dressed stone building put up by the grain merchant Roger Marley in 1839. He also built the adjoining houses along the left side of Bridge Street. In the early 1900s a descendent, Mary Josephine Marley, bequeathed the property to St Patrick's Church, which in turn sold it to Mr Charles Conlon in 1955. In 1992, as part of a refurbishment, the left side of the building was demolished and rebuilt, and the right hand side refurbished. To compliment the date stone 'RM – 1839', another marked 'CC – 1992' commemorates the later work.

Portadown Bowling Club started in 1932 (the Cumberland turf having been laid in 1930) and its ground is seen here in the summer of 1938. The shelter at the far end of the green was in the adjacent Pleasure Gardens, surrounded by swings and a see-saw. It was demolished in the 1960s. Through the years the club and individual members have won many tournaments and championships, but none yet have equalled club member William J. Rosbotham's achievement of 1954. With the Northern Ireland team at the British Empire and Commonwealth Games in Vancouver, Rosbotham and his partner Percy J. Watson won gold in the pairs. The Canadians took silver and the Scots bronze. In 1997 club members Ian Perry and Andrew Hughes won the Irish Pairs Championship at Belmont, Belfast.

Bridge Street, Edenderry, flanked by the bridge over the River Bann which is just out of sight to the left, and Moffatt's Art Studio, at the corner of Watson Street, on the right. The chimney of Portadown Foundry stands in the background. The foundry is gone, but their cast iron fenders, with the logo 'Portadown Foundry Ltd', still protect base walls at vehicular entrances. Nestling between the terraced housing, which dates from the 1840s, stands the 1st Presbyterian Church which was built in 1858 to replace one which had been erected in 1822 when the congregation moved from a house in High Street where the Ulster Bank now stands. John C. Hoy, the butcher and fish merchant next to the church, is still trading.

THE BRIDGE, PORTADOWN.

The first attempt to bridge the Bann at Portadown was with a primitive wooden structure which was built in the 1630s but destroyed a decade later in the Civil War. Successors were similarly short-lived until the existing granite bridge was built in 1834. However, it traversed a dry riverbed as by that time the river had been diverted. In 1922, as part of an unemployment relief scheme aimed at ex-servicemen, the carriageway over the bridge was widened from 28 feet 10 inches to 56 feet 5 inches. It is hoped that by 2004 the bridge will be replaced by a modern structure. This mid-1920s view from the right bank shows Bridge Street extending out towards Edenderry, with Sam Bacci's café and chip shop, now closed, on the left.

Thomas A. Shillington was a wood merchant and his quay and warehouse on the left bank of the river, a few hundred yards downstream of the Bann Bridge, date from the early 1830s. This 1918 photograph shows a line of barges, one having unloaded wood (the 1905 Ordnance Survey map shows the building as a sawmill) onto the quayside, while another is being unloaded with a barge-mounted derrick. The warehouse has survived, occupied by Haldane and Fisher, builders' merchants, although the basin is now gone. In the 1970s the little harbour was filled and leveled to form a car park. The houses through the opening onto Castle Street still stand, but not Calvin's flour mill, with its distinctive square brick chimney, which came down in the 1960s.

THE BRIDGE AND RIVER BANN, PORTADOWN.

This 1912 view shows Portadown as a busy inland port with the barges, or lighters, which plied along the Newry Canal between Belfast and Newry. This important link, which opened in 1742, a century before the railway, brought not only the raw materials to allow the town to grow as an industrial centre, but served as a conduit for its produce. Through the central arch of the bridge Shillington's Quay can just be seen.

The bridge carrying the A3 Northway over the Bann and onto Armagh. The early 1970s brought a period of transition and change and road development swept away much of the old town. The railway line runs by the bridge's northern side. On the opposite bank sits Portadown Foundry in the appropriately named Foundry Street, off Bridge Street.

Portadown Boat Club was rowing the River Bann, from a boathouse on the right bank, for sometime before its official founding in 1877 and by 1903 had elevated its annual regatta (still held each May) to an event on the Portadown calendar. The club's colours, amber and green, derive from the Bann Lily which grows profusely along the riverbank in summer. The photograph shows the club team – H.L. Bell, 2nd; Sydney Bright, Bow; Jack A. Wilson, Stroke; George Dougan, 3rd; and Samuel Wilson, Cox – which won the Metropolitan Grand Challenge Cup for coxed fours at the Dublin Metropolitan Regatta held on 23 and 24 June 1904. The one and a quarter mile race was the Blue Riband of Irish rowing. Started in 1869, the regatta was held at Ringsend in the Port of Dublin, then Islandbridge and now at Blessington. The club is still working at emulating that success (don't tell them it was rowed over

Portadown Boat Club -04. Winners of The Metropolitan Cup. (The blue ribbon of Irish rowing)

in 2001 by the Old Collegians of Dublin). In later years at least three of the crew served the people of the community. While Dr George Dougan tended their health (and chaired the District War Memorial Committee), Jack Wilson arranged their funerals and Sidney Bright, solicitor, wound up their estates.

A coxed four rowing the Bann; maybe they were hoping to emulate the 1904 success at Dublin! The message on the postcard on which this picture from 1908 appeared, sent to Scott the grocer at 53–55 Donegal Road, Belfast, suggests hard times in Portadown – 'send us along by return a couple of boxes of custard'!

EDENDERRY, PORTADOWN

Edenderry in the 1930s. Bridge Street runs off to the left towards Lurgan Road, while to the right Carrickblacker Road leads to Killicomaine and Gilford Road. Ellis's Pub stood on the junction until the 1970s, when it was modernized and became the Tavern Bar.

ALBERT WILSON AND HIS "NIGHTLIGHTS" DANCE BAND, PORTADOWN

Formed in 1932, Albert Wilson and the Nightlights made the Savoy Restaurant's ballroom in West Street *the place* in Portadown for dances and weddings. Albert was the Savoy's catering manager. Although it was used to publicise the Savoy, the photograph was taken in Carlton Street Orange Hall in 1936. This was where the band first played and pictured are George Cassidy, saxophone, Jack McKeag, piano accordion, Eric Jones, drums, Albert Wilson, saxophone, Albert Anderson, double bass, and Jim Wilson (Albert's brother) on trumpet. All were from Portadown, except Jack McKeag who was from Lurgan. Not available for the photograph was trumpeter John Scarlett. They played throughout the war and into the 1950s, except Jim Wilson who joined the Royal Air Force and served as a sergeant. A wireless operator/air gunner, twenty-two year old Jim was on a training flight through the mountains near Llandudno on 19 July 1942 when the aircraft crashed, killing all on board. Albert died in 1977.

PORTADOWN. PIPE. BAND.

Founded in 1928 by Billy Milsop, Robert Jones and Isaac Hannah, Portadown Pipe Band was one of sixteen pipe bands in the greater Portadown area. Hard hours of practice in the Temperance Hall in West Street brought them success in 1947 when they won the annual Northern Ireland Championship. In this photograph, taken at Tandragee during the VE Day celebrations in May 1945, memory has recalled the following names – *front row* (left to right): unknown, unknown, Isaac Hannah, unknown, Ephram Martin, Robert Jones, unknown, Milton Boyle, Harry Jones and Bertie Greer; *back row*: ? Aldrid (first name unknown), unknown, Albert Greenaway, Jimmy Hall, Billy Harrison the drum major, unknown, Billy Milsop and Tom Best. Many others contributed their talents over the seventy years of the band's existence. The back of the photograph is inscribed – 'Auntie, this is Milton's band – he is sitting second from the right. Nothing would do him but I would send you one. Sarah.'

West Street looking towards the town centre, with Henry Street on the left and the houses in Atkinson Street beyond the railway bridge parapet to the right. The Northway road development of the early 1970s changed this scene just a little! Whether the photographer drew the children's interest, or vice versa, we cannot know, but the girls in their smocks, and the boys in their knickerbockers – and so many shoeless – make an interesting study of Edwardian children's dress. The man with the horse and cart is thought to be Holmes, the street sweeper, who lived at Killicomaine with his brothers.

A herd of cattle wend their way along Armagh Road to the Saturday market on the Fair Green. The photograph dates from the 1920s – St Mark's Memorial Tower, then being built, would soon appear on the skyline. The prominent domed building on the left is Carleton House which was put up in 1897/98 by Miss Kate Carleton of Gilford Castle. She presented it to the town on 19 December 1917 as a maternity and child welfare centre. It was in use until Craigavon Area Hospital opened in 1972, after which it served as a nurses home until converted into flats in 1993 by Craigavon and District Housing Association (now South Ulster Housing Association). Over the years the street itself has changed little; it is now tarmacadamed and cattle, of course, are much less common.

Carleton Street was dominated by the white facade of the old St Marks Church Hall on the left (since demolished and rebuilt in red brick) and the then newly built front to the three-storey Orange hall to the right. Although work commenced on the Orange hall in 1873, it did not open until April 1882. The accommodation soon proved inadequate and had to be extended and was given a new facade. The largest of Portadown's six Orange halls, it accommodated twenty-five lodges and preceptory organizations. For the duration of the Second World War it was requisitioned by the War Office for army use.

This laboratory in 'Portadown Ladies School' was actually within Miss Kennedy's Carleton Collegiate on Armagh Road, and taken, as noted on the blackboard, on 6 December 1910. Despite earning a fine reputation in Portadown's education community, Miss Kennedy closed the school when she married a few years later. The chemical equation on the blackboard reads '$NH_4NO_3 = N_2O + 2H_2O$', i.e. when the white soluble crystalline salt Ammonium Nitrate is heated to 169.6 °C it yields Nitrous Oxide and water. Nitrous Oxide is otherwise known as laughing gas, although from the sober faces it looks as if they had only just started the experiment!

With the growth of industrialisation in Portadown at the end of the nineteenth century, the need for a school that could prepare young people for industrial work was satisfied with the opening of the Technical School on Armagh Road in 1902. Built in 1900 as a short-lived Cholera Hospital, the blackstone building was converted to an eight classroom school. The hospital's floor drainage system and white tiling survive in at least one room. By 1917 it was a 'Day Commercial School' with five full-time and eight part-time teachers. In 1935, this original facade was lost behind a new brick and mortar edifice. What became of the lads, or their contribution to the town's prosperity, is unknown. The college remained on this site until 1977, when, as Portadown College of Further Education, it moved to a new building on Lurgan Road.

Although officially founded in 1924 when they were admitted to the senior league, Portadown Football and Athletic Club has played at Shamrock Park on Brownstown Road since the 1890s, when it was the County Armagh Agricultural Society's showground. The club bought the ground in the 1950s (after the stand shown here was rebuilt following a fire in 1949). With no small help from internationalist David Cochrane, who went on to play for Leeds, they won the Gold Cup in 1933, but took almost sixty years to reach their best season – 1991 – when they were Irish League Champions and swept up the Irish Cup, the Ulster Cup and the Budweiser Cup. This photograph probably dates from the 1920s – is anybody able to name any of the team?

Born in Co. Cavan, Edward James Saunderson spent his formative years in France, returning to Ireland in 1858 as a twenty-one year old to manage the family estate. After receiving a commission in the Cavan Militia, 4th Battalion Royal Irish Fusiliers, he gained the rank of colonel. Elected Liberal MP for Cavan in 1865, he later broke with Gladstone's party over church disestablishment and joined the Conservatives. His parliamentary life's work was resistance to Parnell's Home Rule Bill and he famously asserted that 'the Home Rule Bill may pass this House, but it will never pass the bridge at Portadown'. Within two years of joining the Orange Order in 1882 he was Deputy Grand Master, and became Grand Master for Ireland in 1901. Winning the North Armagh seat (containing Portadown) in 1885, he held it and the leadership of the Parliamentary Unionists until his death on 21 October 1906.

Within weeks of Colonel Saunderson's passing a public subscription was opened to raise a memorial to him. A commanding site before the parish church at the head of Market Street was chosen. Sculpted by Sir William Goscombe John, R.A. (1860–1952), the bronze casting was made by A.B. Burton, brass founders of Thames Ditton in Surrey, whose history extended back to the late seventeenth century. Other statues cast at this foundry included those of Robert Burns in George Square, Glasgow, Robert Peel in Parliament Square, London, and Captain James Cook in Sydney, Australia.

The statue was unveiled on Tuesday, 29 March 1910. This carriage, pictured at Woodhouse Street, was carrying the speakers for the ceremony. In the coach was Mr Walter Hume Long (1854–1924), MP for South Dublin and chairman of the Irish Unionist Parliamentary Party, who would perform the unveiling, and he was accompanied by the Marquis of Londonderry, the Earl of Erne and others. Local luminaries who also attended the occasion included D.G. Shillington, Major Blacker and Dr George Dougan.

Such was Saunderson's popularity that a crowd of 30,000, some viewing from hired vantage points in upper storey windows, attended the unveiling of his statue. Sir Edward Carson, who could not attend, said in a letter which was read out that 'he never knew a more loyal friend, nor a greater gentleman'. Among the crowd can be seen representatives of government, the army and the Orange Order.

For the seventh anniversary of the Armistice, Lieut. General Sir Travers Clarke unveiled the Portadown and district war memorial at a dedication service which commenced at noon on Friday 13 November 1925. Of the 321 officers and men named on the memorial, all but 123 of them had served with the county regiment, the Royal Irish Fusiliers. Unusually they are listed street by street for the town, and by area for the countryside. The Irish granite pedestal is surmounted by the angel of peace tending a wounded soldier amongst the battlefield debris of sandbags and gas masks. Colonel Saunderson on his plinth, who had held the centre ground in front of the church since 1910, was moved a little to the right. Sixty-six names were added after the Second World War, while a small grey granite stone, erected in 1992, commemorates men of the Ulster Defence Regiment. Portadown's first casualty of the Second World War was Seaman James Whitla of the Royal Navy, who was lost with 579 others when the aircraft carrier HMS *Courageous* was sunk in the Atlantic by a U-boat on 18 September 1939. His name is listed on a memorial at Plymouth Hoe, but it was only in June 2001 that his name was added to the Portadown memorial.

Dan Winter's Cottage at Loughgall, the recognised birthplace of the Orange Order. Following the Battle of the Diamond at Diamond Hill on 21 September 1795, Daniel Winter, James Wilson and James Sloan met here to form the Order as a defensive organisation. This photograph from the early 1900s shows Winter's great-grandson, Robert Winter (1859–1922), seated with a pedlar who had come by. In the left foreground a hen inspects the pedlar's wares. Following extensive renovation, the cottage, which is still owned by the Winter family, was reopened as a museum in September 2000.

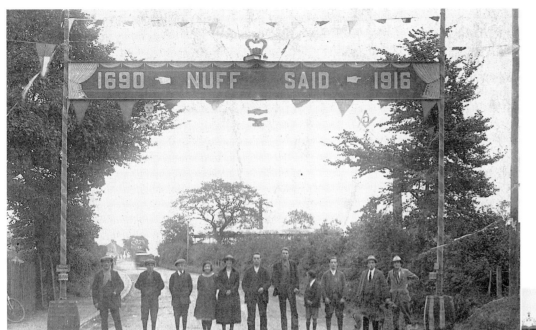

From the First World War period, this enigmatic banner seems to make a connection between 1690 and 1916. The war, in which over three hundred Portadown men would be lost, had reduced the number of the Orange Order's demonstrations – so why this banner? Of the hundreds of townsmen who enlisted in 1914, most joined the 9th Battalion Royal Irish Fusiliers under the command of Lieut. Col. Stewart Blacker and had the tragic misfortune to be involved in the slaughter at the Battle of the Somme which began on 1 July 1916. The fact that the Battle of the Boyne is now celebrated on 12 July, when it was actually fought on 1 July 1692, is due to the change from the Julian to the Gregorian calendar in 1752, when 2 September became 13 September. By this reckoning, 1 July was a significant date.

This 1953 photograph shows the new Edgarstown Orange Arch, dedicated to Sir Edward Carson, QC (1854–1935), Conservative MP for Dublin University between 1892 and 1918, and Duncairn, Belfast, between 1918 and 1921. This arch replaced one of 1937. Thirty feet high and 50 feet wide, its five arches spanned the street and almost swallowed up Barratt the draper. At the last minute, the dedication to 'One King' had to be rewritten as 'One Queen'. It contained many pieces from the old arch and in 1991, when it was superseded by its successor in Margaret Street, many of the adornments were again retained.

It is 1937 and Portadown Orange District are parading up High Street from the railway station and making for Carlton Street on their return from the Twelfth demonstrations at Lurgan. Portadown had been the 1935 venue. Heading the parade on the white horse is Tom Dermott of Lodge 18 Golden Springs, Brackagh, who was a mechanic and welder at McHugh's Garage in Edward Street. From the outbreak of the Second World War horses were no longer used in parades. Although the goat forms a small part of Orange tradition, this stray had no part in the procession other than an accidental walk-on part.

MOYALLON COTTAGES SHOWING NEW SCHOOL, MOYALLON, PORTADOWN.

Some three miles out of town on the Gilford Road sits Moyallon, pictured here in the late nineteenth century. Opposite lies the estate of the linen magnate, John Grubb Richardson (1813–1890), who built these cottages, and the schoolhouse (the first of three schools including the present one) to the left of them, for his estate workers. A Quaker and philanthropist, Richardson built a model village for his mill workers at Bessbrook, but plans to repeat his munificence at Moyallon for agricultural workers did not come to fruition. The school is now a dwellinghouse and the cottages, one of which served as an orphanage, are still inhabited.

From the early 1910s until the 1930s, the charabanc (the name derives from the French *char-a-banc,* i.e. a carriage with benches) was popular for summer outings and day trips. Probably owned by the Portadown-based Irish Road Motors, this fleet would have been heading for the coast with staff from a Portadown factory or department store.

A group of youngsters, pictured in the early 1920s on a summer's afternoon outing, pose beside one of the two streams which then coursed through Peoples Park. Bounded by Obins Street, Park Road and Garvaghy Road, the park once lay within the curtilage of Obins Castle. During the Second World War, community air raid shelters (one of which has survived) were built there and other areas were given to allotments as part of the 'Dig for Victory' effort.

Branching from Carrickblacker Road, Bachelor's Walk runs towards Seagoe through the one-time estate of Eden Villa. Now derelict, the estate was the home of the Atkinson family for whom Atkinson Avenue, off West Street, was named. Thomas Joyce Atkinson, a thirty-eight year old major in the Royal Irish Fusiliers was killed on the Somme on 1 July 1916. The cottage at the entrance was at one time home to the McCabe family.

Bachelor's Walk, Portadown

Seagoe's old world charm vanished in the late 1940s with the widening of this road which swept away the cottages and brought the prefabs of Seagoe Park to the meadow opposite. One of Ireland's oldest Christian settlements, possibly dating from AD 540, the name Seagoe derives from the Latin *Sedes Gobhani*, or 'the House of Saint Gobhan' which, over centuries of use, became 'Seagoe'. The saint is also remembered in the town's Gobhan Street. The roofless church building marked on a map of 1609 was rebuilt, but destroyed in 1641 and repaired in 1669 by Valentine Blacker of Manor House, Ballynaghie. The foundation stone of the present church was laid on the new site (the old burial ground having become overcrowded) on 1 June 1814.